Trains

Chris Oxlade

Heinemann LIBRARY

www.heinemann.co.uk
Visit our website to find out more information about Heinemann Library books.

To order:
 Phone 44 (0) 1865 888066
 Send a fax to 44 (0) 1865 314091
Visit the Heinemann Bookshop at www.heinemann.co.uk to browse our catalogue and order online.

First published in Great Britain by Heinemann Library, Halley Court, Jordan Hill, Oxford OX2 8EJ a division of Reed Educational and Professional Publishing Ltd.
Heinemann is a registered trademark of Reed Educational & Professional Publishing Ltd.

OXFORD MELBOURNE AUCKLAND
JOHANNESBURG BLANTYRE GABORONE
IBADAN PORTSMOUTH (NH) USA CHICAGO

Designed by Paul Davies and Associates
Originated by Ambassador Litho Ltd
Printed in Hong Kong/China

05 04 03 02 01
10 9 8 7 6 5 4 3 2 1

ISBN 0431 10853 6

British Library Cataloguing in Publication Data

Oxlade, Chris
Trains. – (Transport around the world)
1.Railroads – Trains – Juvenile literature
2.Railroads – Juvenile literature 3.Railroad travel – Juvenile literature
I.Title
625.2

Acknowledgements
The Publishers would like to thank the following for permission to reproduce photographs:
R D Battersby p16; Steve Benbow p14; Sylvia Cordaiy pp7, 8, 10, 23, 27; Eye Ubiquitous pp4, 6, 11, 17, 24; James Davis Travel Photography p18; Milepost p25; PA Photos p15; Pictures p13; QA Photos p20; Quadrant pp12, 21, 26; SNCF p19; Tony Stone Images pp5, 9; TRH Pictures p28; VSOE p22; Science Photo Library p29

Cover photograph reproduced with permission of Quadrant Pic

Every effort has been made to contact copyright holders of any material reproduced in this book. Any omissions will be rectified in subsequent printings if notice is given to the Publisher.

Contents

Any words appearing in the text in bold, **like this**, are explained in the glossary.

What is a train?

A train is a machine that moves along on metal rails. Passengers travel inside the train's **carriages**. The carriages are pulled along by a **locomotive**. A train can have many carriages or just a few.

A train driver sits in a small **cab** at the front of the locomotive. The driver makes the train start and stop, and speed up and slow down by moving handles and pedals.

How trains work

This is an **electric** train. Electric motors in the **locomotive** make its wheels turn round to move the train along. The electricity comes from wires above the track.

This is a **diesel** locomotive. It has a huge **engine** called a diesel engine that turns its wheels. The engine needs **fuel** to make it work.

Old trains

Early trains used **steam** for power. The first steam **locomotive** was called the *Rocket*. It was built in 1829 and carried passengers between Liverpool and Manchester in England.

8

Monster steam locomotives like this one had very powerful **engines**. They pulled **freight** trains with hundreds of wagons of **cargo** across the United States in the 1940s.

Steam trains

In some countries trains are still pulled by **steam locomotives**. Inside the locomotive, a roaring fire makes water boil to make steam.

On a steam locomotive, steam makes
pistons move in and out. Long rods
attached to the pistons make the wheels
spin round.

Where are trains used?

Trains can only be used where there is a track laid for them. Most tracks are made up of two metal rails. Coloured lights called signals tell train drivers when to stop or go.

Railway tracks go between towns and cities where there are railway stations. Passenger trains stop at stations to let passengers get on and off.

Trains to work

Every day millions of people travel to work and school on **commuter** trains. These trains stop at most stations, picking up passengers and taking them into city centres.

Commuter trains have lots of wide doors so that the passengers can get on and off quickly. Inside the **carriages** there is space for passengers to stand if all the seats are taken.

Trains underground

Underground trains travel through tunnels deep beneath the busy city streets. The stations they stop at are also underground. All underground trains are **electric** trains.

Underground trains avoid the busy traffic above ground. They can get very crowded during the rush hour. Inside the **carriages** there are plenty of handles for standing passengers to hold on to.

Express trains

Express trains whizz along at more than 200 kilometres per hour. They carry people quickly between cities. This express train is the famous Japanese 'bullet train'.

18

This is the front of an express train. It has a smooth, **streamlined** shape. This lets the train slice easily through the air as it speeds along.

Shuttle trains

A shuttle carries cars and coaches through the Channel Tunnel between England and France. Other wagons carry trucks through the tunnel.

Passengers drive their cars on to the shuttle at one end of the tunnel. They can stay in their cars on the train. They drive off again when the train reaches the other end.

Luxury trains

RANDS EXPRESS EUROPEEN

VENICE SIMPLON-ORIENT

Some long distance trains are very **luxurious**. Passengers have their own **cabins** to sleep in overnight. This train is the famous Orient Express which travels through Europe and Asia.

On a luxury train the passengers eat their meals in a special **carriage** called a dining car. It is like a restaurant on wheels. Meals are cooked in part of the car called the galley.

Freight trains

A **freight** train carries **cargo** instead of passengers. The cargo is carried in special wagons. Each wagon is connected to the next one with a hook called a coupling.

24

Railway tracks are built on a layer of small pieces of rock called ballast. Special freight wagons can spread new ballast when it is needed. A hole in the bottom of the wagon opens to let the ballast out.

Mountain trains

Mountain trains can go up much steeper hills than other trains. This train is climbing a mountain railway in the Alps in Switzerland.

Mountain railway tracks have a rack between the rails. **Locomotives** have an extra wheel that fits into the rack. It stops the train sliding back down the steep track.

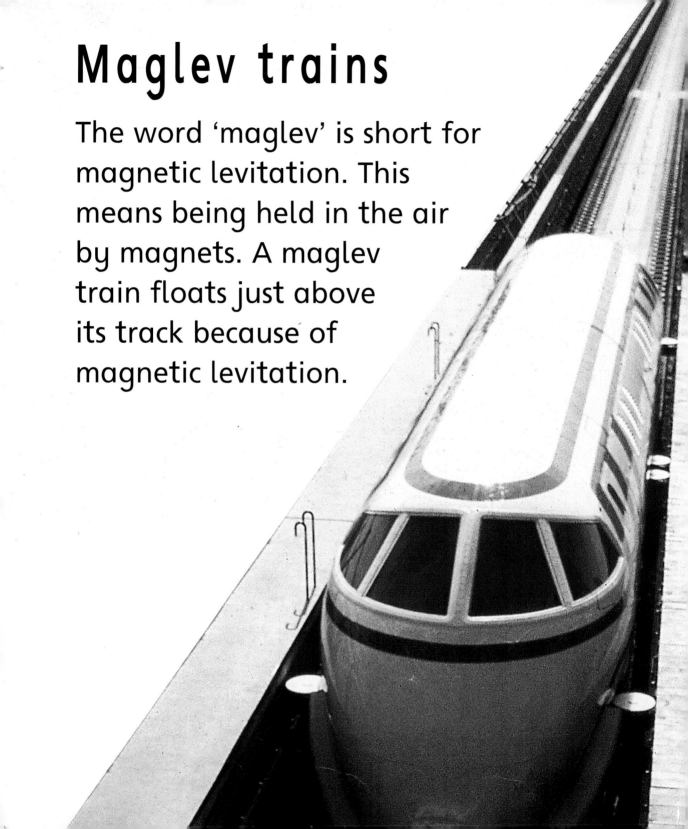

Maglev trains

The word 'maglev' is short for magnetic levitation. This means being held in the air by magnets. A maglev train floats just above its track because of magnetic levitation.

There are very strong magnets in a
maglev track and train. They push
against each other. This forces the train
upwards and forwards. Maglev trains
are fast and quiet.

Timeline

1803 British engineer Richard Trevithick builds the first **steam locomotive**. It pulls wagons around an iron-making factory.

1808 The *Clermont* carries passengers along rivers in the USA. It is the first boat powered by a steam **engine**.

1830 The first passenger railway is opened in England between Liverpool and Manchester. The trains are pulled by a steam locomotive called the *Rocket*.

1863 The world's first underground railway is opened in London.

1879 The first **electric** locomotive is demonstrated in Berlin.

1883 The luxury train the *Orient Express* makes its first journey between Paris, France and Istanbul, Turkey.

1940s Enormous *Big Boy* locomotives are built in the USA for pulling cargo trucks. Each one weighed 600 tonnes.

1981 In France the TGV express train makes its first journey between Paris and Lyon.

1982 A maglev railway is opened at Birmingham airport, England.

Glossary

cab	the space at the front of a locomotive where the train driver sits
cabin	a private room on a train with beds for passengers
cargo	goods that are moved from place to place
carriage	a long vehicle that rolls along a railway track with seats for passengers
commuter	a person who travels to work by car or train
diesel	type of engine that needs fuel to run
electric	using electricity to run
engine	a machine that powers movement using fuel
freight	cargo transported by train or ship
fuel	a substance that burns to make heat
locomotive	a vehicle with an engine or motor that pulls carriages or wagons along a railway track
luxurious	very comfortable
piston	a rod that moves in and out of a cylinder
steam	water that has become a gas
streamlined	curved and smooth

Index

Titles in the *Transport Around The World* series

Hardback   0 431 10840 4

Hardback   0 431 10841 2

Hardback   0 431 10839 0

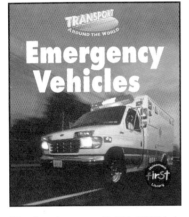

Hardback   0 431 10854 4

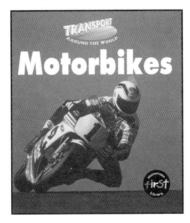

Hardback   0 431 10852 8

Hardback   0 431 10838 2

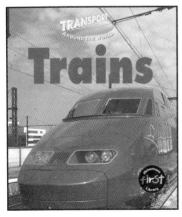

Hardback   0 431 10853 6

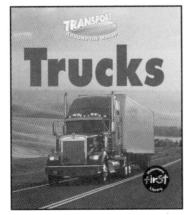

Hardback   0 431 10855 2

Find out about the other titles in this series on our website www.heinemann.co.uk/library